The Ravens Will Arrive Later

Praise for *The Ravens Will Arrive Later*

The prodigious poet Jonathan Yungkans' earthbound ravens take metaphorical-magical flight and land masterfully, properly placed upon the pages of this enlightened collection of fine narrative poetry.

> Joan Jobe Smith, author of *Jehovah Jukebox* and *Moonlight A-Go-Go*

You read through it the first time noticing the long titles and long lines, and just the inherent goodness of it all, and then you begin to catch the ghost echoes that intertwine the various poems like dry leaves skittering in a chill wind. And you wonder if it's a reverse ghost—a corporeal body walking within a void, or are you just dreaming your way through it. But no, it's more solid than that. Re-read, and fold yourself into the wonder. Drawing with a black pen the contours of watercolor, reinvented in language. Solid and ethereal at the same time. So many of these poems are epic in scope, should be the centerpiece of some other book—but here they just fit softly into their assigned corner within the shape of it all. I would like to give you a name to hang on to, a reference to position it, but this is new. These winding sheets wrapped around a brain are unique to Yungkans, and he gives you this book as a gift. Remember—memories are meant to be glared at.

> Paul Ilechko, author of *Fragmentation and Volta*

In *The Ravens Will Arrive Later*, Jon Yungkans explores everything from social and political realities to personal despair, from art history to pop culture, with a genuine, intelligent, and humane voice that cuts through darkness with wit and ironic humor, arriving just in time.

> Clint Margrave, author of *Visitor*

The Ravens Will Arrive Later
Copyright © 2025 Jonathan Yungkans

Cover Art by Gnashing Teeth Publishing

The font used is Times New Roman
The cover font is Abolition

All rights reserved. No duplication or reuse of any selection is allowed without the express written consent of the publisher.

        Gnashing Teeth Publishing
        242 East Main Street
        Norman AR 71960
        http://GnashingTeethPublishing.com

Printed in the United States of America

ISBN 978-1-966075-25-7

Non-Fiction: Poetry

Gnashing Teeth Publishing First Edition

For William Mohr, who always pushed me toward something better.

TABLE OF CONTENTS

Make Nice, Like You Really Cared _____ 1

Appearances Must Be Kept Up at Whatever Cost Until the Day of
Judgment and Afterward If Possible _____ 2

And Toward the Center a Vacancy One Knew _____ 3

Pondering a Theorem: What You Said a Hotel Was _____ 6

Only the Frozen Emphasis _____ 8

It Belongs to Each of Us Like a Blanket _____ 11

There Are Always Those Who Think You Ought To _____ 15

I Shovel All the Things You Want to Hear _____ 16

Batman Came Out and Clubbed Me _____ 18

Let's Take a Commercial Break Here _____ 19

A Surreal Intimacy, Like Jazz Music _____ 20

No One Has the Last Laugh _____ 21

    1. With No Apologies to the World or the Ether _____ 21

    2. Yet Not So Dirty, Surely Not in the Spiritual Sense, _____ 21

    3. The Whole Other Issue of Belonging _____ 22

    4. Just So You Know, This Is the Falling-Off Place _____ 22

Birds Make Poor Role Models _____ 23

Like the Scream of the Rising Moon _____ 24

Followed by Periods of Silence Which Get Shorter and Shorter _____ 25

We See One Thing Next to Another _____ 26

There Is No Indication This Will Happen _____ 29

We All Came to Be Here Quite Naturally	31
Like the Cubist Diary of a Brook	34
It Must Mean I'm Not Here Yet	37
Our Quondam Companions Persist	38
This Future Does Us Good ("Lawful and Proper")	39
Supposing That You Are a Wall	40
The Lady of Shalott's in Hot Water Again	42
Hence It Ends Up with a Scenario of Them All Getting Paid	44
There Had Never Been a Problem with the Water Before	49
Waiters Encourage Us, and Squirrels	52
Pierced Full of Holes by the Evil That Is Not Evil	54
Acknowledgements	57
About the Author	59

Make Nice, Like You Really Cared

Museum patrons take care, whispering into Van Gogh's cloned ear—
a copy of one he left in a reddening handkerchief
for someone he hoped might make nice

and listen like she really cared, desperation glowing like a cigarette

before taking off her clothes, hoping she'd make nice
after sex instead of sitting draped in sullen silence and bed sheets,
cigarette dangling between her lips,

like she really cared, a thread of words in blue smoke out of reach

making nice not drifting close
before she shoos him out the door so she can get to her next john,
like she really cared, because money's only so green,

and making nice with conversation's money browning into autumn,

a dry leaf skittering in a chill wind—
and decades after that woman stopped taking Van Gogh's money,
museum patrons making nice

in the hope a person sooner or later feels while trying to make nice,

and listen,
even if it's a disembodied auricle suspended in clear gel,
a computer processing words into nerve impulses—

caring like a priest's voice though the lattice inside a confessional,

or a model talking like she really cared
while the artist makes nice, trying to work,
stabbing the canvas in minute, hasty brush strokes,

making nice to impart the illusion of something like a holy mood.

Appearances Must Be Kept Up at Whatever Cost Until the Day of Judgment and Afterward If Possible

Smile and say nothing whenever possible.
Otherwise, people will think I'll explode
and be sprayed with bone fragments
and pieces of my mind I should have kept to myself.
And who wants all that coming at them from behind a service desk,
a bank counter,
a check stand that wasn't safely self-checkout,
wanting nothing more than to smile and say nothing themselves
and stay stressed and miserable,
depressed and miserable,
not hearing their kids screaming and quietly miserable?

You're picking up a theme here, right?
Neurodivergent
means diverging from where people want to stay sad but quiet.
Watching the parade go by with a poker face.
And I come by as Winnie-the-Pooh
voiced by Sterling Holloway in an old animated film,
singing, "I'm just that little old black rain cloud."
I'm paddling through their troubled waters
because I couldn't take the fucking bridge for the life of me
by keeping my mouth shut.
And the reek from the water is turning their stomachs and minds.

I get hung up on principle like it's a nail in my shoe
and I'm saying, "Jesus fuck, I'm bleeding."
The other person looks down
and sees a crimson puddle between my grey Skechers slip-on
and the grey slab that passes as a floor
or the bottom of a lake.
They see a reflection
and look up at me
with an expression on their face
as easy to read as the front-page headline of a newspaper,
saying, *Couldn't you just keep moving?*

And Toward the Center a Vacancy One Knew

I've been a shadow some time now. Could attribute a virus
for lingering in one spot, moldering into the floor. Depression
gave 20 years practice to hover like smoke, to avoid sunlight

so it wouldn't spotlight me like a dust mote suspended midair.
Better to blend, noiseless and indistinguishable from the dark.
I wanted that much to disappear, vacate into myself, avoiding

mirrors like a person never peering outside a window to check
for rain. Covid locked those habits, threw a deadbolt, sat me
with them on the front porch to blend with shade, watch the door.

></br>
> On the paper's front page, a pedestrian
> strides Grand Avenue, a reverse ghost—
> a corporeal body walking within a void
> —like the rest of the *Whittier Daily News*.
> Air is detained in black type, caught
>
> and hermetically sealed in white space.
> Glass wall mirrors a vacant Los Angeles.
> City Hall's pyramid spire sphinxes me
> into a three-part riddle whose questions
> I don't recognize. The atmosphere ebbs.

They stopped making front doors like this three generations ago.
Almost square, wide enough to drive a pick-up truck through.
Its brick or scab red paint reminds me of Civil War iron armor;

its oaken composure predates tall pines adjacent to this house.
It's a comfort to see something more substantial than myself.
I eavesdrop for brass tumblers to turn, swallow and breathe in.

Movement restricted in state, the paper reads. *Travelling allowed for food and medical care and to get exercise.* As if anyone dared to give their fears a stroll. No wind. Not a sign of squirrels or jays.

                              I don't know why the riddle is a stranger.
                              If I'm just a hermit, hermetically sealed.
                              Whether there's just one sphinx or two,
                              not facing the mirror to dodge the second,
                              pass on meeting questions about myself.

                              Covid's not the only virus that suffocates.
                              What to do with a mind that's born sick?
                              When neighbors, ordered to stay at home,
                              watch contagion unfold through windows,
                              distant before distancing became sociable.

Green and green and green, down winding road and college quad—
Philadelphia Street void of brotherly love, rolling toward Uptown,
Whittier College's dorms unconversational. Not even the specter

of favorite son Richard Nixon is in sight. Never thought to miss
his black-suited gloom when he'd haunt his alma mater, across
the street and a turn toward the quad. Much as I enjoy the birds

who now punctuate this noiseless sentence of cement sidewalks
on a street that meanders like a passage from a Faulkner novel,
there's something about the lack of faces along its solitary green.

                              I glance toward the door, see blood
                              in cracks through my chapped hands,
                              washed every trip, regardless of what
                              wasn't touched. I eye the pedestrian
                              in the paper, walking, and recognize

                              the figure as myself. Our reflection,
                              passing the looking-glass, is trapped
                              between microscope slides, catches
                              the sick, not the sickness. Conflates
                              the two, now three, in a mutual face.

Back inside the house, the safety of desk, laptop. A video posted
of fingers tracing Bach's Goldberg aria on a piano. Hands echo
in the instrument's polished fall board. Yellow drapes. A window.

Only the pianist's hands are visible—measured, exact as phrases
they articulate—enough resonance to assuage the ear, enough
image to assure the mind that isolate is not necessarily alone—

a nighttime promise to wake from sleep. I watch and watch the video,
for Bach and not for Bach, the rippling a comfort,
like finches and sparrows outside, like finches and sparrows, the hushed
outside.

Pondering a Theorem: What You Said a Hotel Was

1

Browning maple leaves pile along corridor sides, along which a doorway leads to a large, vacant room filled with gym equipment. Tendrils stretch down a wall of windows. They lengthen as I watch, while I climb on a stair stepper, going nowhere. Do I climb to escape my thoughts? Or because my thoughts are chasing me? Elongated, deep-green spearpoint leaves, ribbed with thin black lines. Purple, star-shaped buds appear at the ends of tendrils. They blossom. Drop through glass, onto carpet. Already limp, the flowers are fragile as snowflakes. Gifts to cheer me up? Something poisonous from inside my ears?

2

Between white powder-finish walls, conversations rattle plaster until the red bricks beneath vibrate in mortar. Given the chance, that masonry would probably hum. Upstairs, curtains hang with a negligée's looseness. Polished mahogany bedposts capture what light filters through opaque fabric. Reservations lounge, waiting under bedsheets, lipstick-lipped and bedroom-eyed. How many are masks, other than all, at one time or another? That's the pot calling the kettle beige, but we can discuss it over coffee. Let's rut around in a lie, first, just for old time's sake. I don't care which. Just make sure it feels good for everyone all around.

3

There's only so much vacancy a person can take when he's wheeled into a crowded room, locked inside a glass ideology like Houdini's water-torture chamber. Suspended upside-down, feet in thick wooden stocks. Glass tank filled with water. The band strikes up a tune. While the audience dances around the booth, two ushers place a full-length mirror to face the tank so I can watch my lack of progress in complete isolation. It's like the poem about Buffalo Bill. He shot and broke all those clay pigeons, just like that, then left like a good blue-eyed boy with Mister Death.

4

Half a blue supermoon onward in night's muggy air while hell freezes over. Cement-block walls. Painted Swiss coffee to hide red, green, black streaks that scream, given their birthing pangs as graffiti. Mugging stories we don't want to talk about. Concrete poured to set rebar, bar moisture to start rust. It's only a matter of time. Umber granules—oxidized metal—accumulate in the bottom of an hourglass. Umber or umbrage? The anger in shadows cast by trees? Or simply what's behind a façade, corroding as the aggregate surrounding it breaks down? Eyes follow traces of names, words through weathering paint.

5

I dwell in too many rooms, all at once. Wishing for a place like home that is also an escape. Bed made. Clean sheets. Ocean view into which to drift after a long walk on sand, thinking something cool and aquamarine would crash any moment. A room of yellow roses, butter-yellow wallpaper. Walls of a noun which once meant error, heresy, madness, into which I was born. As if *dwell* could be *dwale*—nightshade in the guise of fresh black coffee. And I will dwell in the lobby of the Lord forever, watching angels pass. To sleep. Perchance to dream.

Only the Frozen Emphasis

The ravens will arrive later, clucking their tongues—
a complex series of clicks and pops more love song
than any expected from dusky feathers, long beaks—
black as red, blue and yellow combined, a shade
more knowing than lack of sunlight.
                                        Birds flock
in their cosmos, their order, to a Scripture's words
in a flapping atmosphere—a sphere of steaming
vowels and consonants. It's all Greek to my ears—
like knowing where doubts will push through skin,
pin feathers in a mind's fledge. Or am I wandering

too far into abstraction—an Icarian over-distance,
between the devil and the deep blue sea—for my
mental flights and crashes to smooth into a parabola
easy for other eyes to trace? Easy in a year locked
and bolted to one spot
                            to wish to fly. But I was born
with a slipstream tracing feathers, a leap through air,
thinking other birds followed my lunges and twists—
follow the metaphor that was synaptic connections,
leaping between neurons in a brain—flight from pole
across a chasm
                    to a sharpened pole. It's Greek to me,
and other birds speak and fly in Latin—a love song
with its complex series of clicks and pops between
phone lines, power poles, and Covid, Covid burning
bright in the forest of our fright, forcing us to wear
masks
     over masks we ply as faces, words as masks
and conversations braided into a lynch rope—more
grave than gravy, to braid Scrooge into rope fiber—
and I mistype *grace* in place of *grave*. How holier
than bird-brained of me. Another brick in the wall
to lob slyward? I meant skyward,
                                  another slip-up—
or was it? A raven has eyes, can recognize faces,
and Freud knew an involuntary sidestep when one

crow-whizzed or raven-glided past him. I've always
seemed an odd duck out—in this world, not of it—
as if people thought me hatched, not born. A joke

that shows my age, perhaps a political incorrectness
toward waterfowl, making others more flappable
and on-the-wing around me—detached, wavering
lines, shortening on their way toward the horizon—
like church folk after service, roosting and clucking

out of earshot, of this world and nowhere inside it
for whatever hatches. Language lain and incubated,
parents waiting for its chicks to hatch, the other shoe
to drop in some unfortunate direction. Bless my heart
and hope it isn't catching—
                            like the bedside manner
of a vaccination center doc who said, in full medical
parlance, on side-effects of my second Covid shot,
"You'll just feel crummy." It wasn't church talk,
but the distance was there and brought Sundays back
like the Aegean rushing to my face—Icarus tumbling,

and the odds-man taking bets on the point of impact,
transparent but tangible as a guy scribbling on a pad
right there, in the church parking lot. Maybe details
for that doc, after a year of patients crashing birdlike
into unseen windows
                    from a virus sudden and hard
as a clear plate loss of breath and heartbeat were too
too close to Twain's summer in San Francisco, all
"White Christmas" and Titanic smacking an iceberg,
blue-white and floating right in the way—a fortress
of solitude misplaced, from the Christopher Reeve

version of sudden calamity after being Superman—
and she was wavering from exposure to kryptonite,
like medical professionals from becoming Superman
during a pandemic longer than Clark Kent's lifetime,
aching down to their bones.
                    Yeah, I jump around—

raven hopping along a eucalyptus branch, hyperactive
to make what feels like an insane flight makes sense,
for my own good—the darkness of corvid feathers
too prominent a display for daylight, and a flight
that perhaps can't be avoided for either life or air.

It Belongs to Each of Us Like a Blanket

Funny how winding sheets wrap around a brain—
quodlibet of the quotidian shroud, no
matter how brief a face appears, an almond

peeled in its pale complexion and oval shape,
quod erat demonstrandum. Sunglasses,
outsized, suggest Dios de los Muertos—

is it Quarma or Queen Death who's wearing them?
Louboutin heels clack as if by quartz movement,
matching a little black Holly Golightly

shrift. Lady's sure as Jesus on His cross to
burn a Turin Shroud quandary into mind.
It's Death's quirk to quadrate all attention,

strut mortality like a runway model,
garment white as cumulous clouds, billowing
modishly. She turns to promenade away,

watching us as quarry. After this, the quench
of linen's touch is quieting as the earth.
Like a face at rest, eyes closed, ghosting the cloth.

                    The Shroud, whether fashion statement for a quick-
                          change Savior or an Owen Warland device
                                to flutter mechanically past disbelief,

                              reposes butterfly-fragile under glass.
                            Available to see by appointment-only.
                        Like the Scripture on life and death in the

                power of the schedule. The Shroud is the card
                    from doctor or mortician, date of reckoning
              penciled in. Don't quibble with the receptionist—

                    she'll make a quo vadis face, lower glasses,
              show moon craters in place of eyes. Quel dommage!
                          Quis custodiet ipsos custodes? Aren't

                    the watchers sufficiently entertained? Shroud's
                         quo warranto—writ for mankind, complete
                         with flash-watermark, Christ as Polaroid.

That image—closed eyes, flowing hair, nose, beard.
Answer as question. Forget how it was made
Quem quareitus? Who am I really

seeking, past quiescent glass—in a mirror?
—to quantify eyes, ears, hairs on a head,
or to qualify whose? How deep do I mourn—

pun that is also a time of day? Pursue
the Savoir or weave myself into flax,
my warp and weft? Quo jure? Quem quarietus?

                       Peel-back negatives of instamatic film
                          reflect, glittery, in the current of a
                    mental stream like flotsam, querling to quell quick-

                    timing thoughts along hallways hospital-white
                              with antiseptic lies. Can a psyche be
                      washed in the Blood of the Lamb to rebirth it

                    from a curse come quasi-fresh from the womb? "That's
                              a miracle, brother. You'd need Lazarus
                       to kick that field goal, and even then the ref—

                    complete with angel wings, striped shirt and whistle—
                         might call that one a foul. Faith isn't football. You
                       can't play it with baseball rules." But the Holy Land's

holiest between the third and fourth rib. "Quis
separabit?" where nails pierced. "Quo animo?"
an illusion of distance. Shroud's a test page.

A bolt of cloth. A bolt which qualifies beams
as a keel while Jesus does the Galilee
Moonwalk in a quickening storm. A bolt to hold

faith together in a starless, roaring sky.
Maybe He was smiling when Peter said, "If it's
You, Lord, bid me come," and bolted his way

onto a walk on the wet side, a wonder,
as if doing so was no quirk, quod erat
faciendum. Would Jesus say, "It's not Me"?

Fashioning a scarf joint. Tapering the ends
of wood so they hold like two hands, interlocking.
Questioning wood-shop wisdom on attaching

lumber end-to-end and have it hold as one
unbreakable beam or plank, no more than trees
are one while remaining separate trunks. Yet

oaks do that. Roots interweave, like quantum phone
switchboard wires in old detective films, plugged in
and out of the board and seemingly tangled

past any casual grasp. Quo animo
belying the lie of distance underground
through their cores' interlaced quiddity. The Shroud

is a scarf, good as beams with ends rabbited,
cut precise, pattern to pattern, to hammer
until the seam doesn't show, to lock in place.

I sit in a tomb quarried into a mountainside,
quiet as a cement slab. Death clacks stiletto steps.
Dawn and mockingbirds. When deep blue light shreds black—

time that's a quiet lung, collapsed, necrotic
even with bird songs quivering, plenty poised
between leaf and branch to twitter about, air

in chests to do so. Daylight's a quale, quashing
worse than muscles and skin wasting away, bones
falling loose at joints. Every morning. I picture

a winding sheet, a body outlined under it
like dents in a discarded soda can.
A questionable outline? And is it true

blood, oxidized past brick-red to ebony?
Questioning makes a quadrature from what curves
at sunrise back to me in the cubature

of a sepulcher—mornings of hard stone walls—
for which someone else died and was wrapped in flax
simply out of care for me. This is enough.

There Are Always Those Who Think You Ought To
    a comedy

Screaming fraud, fraud and Georgia on my mind, Clown thought
he could get his friends to party hearty at the Capitol, a tiny break
and enter to Make America Quake Again—going red hat, red state,
seeing red and so irate. Just had to Stop the Steal
                                           since white's right
and there's nothing more warped than an honest election. In his full
delusion, Clown emboldened well-wishers at a rally down the street
to go whet the tree of Liberty, like Jefferson said—
                                           bleed the nation
pale until it cries Uncle Tom. Preach democracy as truth and justice
soaked in gasoline, which isn't wrongdoing, just a bar call for shots
in a crowded hysteria. *Isn't Black Lives Matter*, the police thought—
let the good folk stamp and rampage, swing some Confederate flags

like baiting a bull to see red. Never mind the blue-bellied majority—
the states who voted blue. Bide time instead of swinging for Biden.
Takes patience and just the right-wing touch to hone anarchy just right
in the land of Stop Them. Look away, look away
                                           and whistle Dixie.
Buy some vinegar shoes and paper stockings, as folks once mangled
those lyrics—folks who never took to white privilege. It's moonshine—
distill your own, bottle it in Mason jars, then go get
                                               rip-roaring drunk
in front of TV, seeing Mexican kids in cages, Blacks shot and choked.
You're special, Clown told the partiers who came to the Capitol rave—
or was it rage? No matter. It was a hell of a time—a big-heart Love-In.
Like Clown said, when it was time for the party to break, "We love you."

I Shovel All the Things You Want to Hear

—and what I shovel is not so much dirt, mulch and manure. For what
makes America great? Acres and acres raven-black with blood mixed

with a femur here, shoulder blade or jawbone there—furrows plowed

in goodness and mercy but intended to steal, kill and enjoy. Gertrude
Stein said there's no really there there, but even if the wheelbarrow's

empty, like John Ashbery said, who knows what'll jump out of there

singing *America, America*, to crown his good in brotherhood from sea
to shining sea. It's a vintage as tasty as Monsanto Roundup's arsenic,

all that glyphosate herbicide for green lawns, brown weeds—runoff

leached into California wine. Doesn't whatever doesn't kill you make
you stronger, or just make grass greener on a conscience's nether side

while it withers weeds? Inquiring minds would really like to know if

if all lies or select ones are better with bacon as they watch browning
sow's ear, wilting pigweed. Got some chilled Chablis. Want a glass?

What I shovel is more like amalgamating concrete—Portland cement,
sand, water mixed in a wheelbarrow—poured, smoothed, given some

appearance of being level (though which historical slights or grudges

can shift to liquify the ground beneath that slab, good luck in the nest
of times—and I meant best, but in the spirit of payback, take my silk

Freudian slip for the egg from which a country hatched). Who knows

when the first crack breaks surface, whether simple lie or a difference
of opinion? And masonry never untruths. It simply lies around, right?

Beneath these bricks is a stone foundation. George Washington might

have had his slaves lay it. Had enough practice surveying land to make
sure his work line kept straight, the wall straighter. What side of Dixon

do you think the mason laid bricks? Balance of blood to lime in mortar

fathering the country? Puts a whole new spin on Uncle Tom when you
toss Sally Hemings between sheets and pages with Thomas Jefferson.

    I'm waiting for morning glories to glorify the rats which live beneath.
    Deep purple, butter-centered blossoms hide their scampering, sharing

    love in the neighborhood, savoring wires and rafters. "The nightmare

    known as morning glory is correctly called field bindweed." Thus says
    The Desert News. Or is it *The Desert Fake News*? We all have to bind

    together, binding migrant boys and girls inside cages. Don't they look

    like deflated party balloons as they sleep under those Mylar blankets?
    Poet at a Zoom open reading claims whiteness is all colors. Whiteness

    is brown, black, yellow and red, all bottled together and called a blend,

    put on a shelf in the liquor aisle. It goes well with pasta and barbacoa,
    and critics laud it, say it pairs beautifully with cultural appropriation—

    the *all colors* no color and itself, threadlike and sharp as window glass,

    while chokeweed dots the lawn. Roundup withers it, knee to each root,
    until it's good and gone and everyone can pretend it was never there—

Batman Came Out and Clubbed Me

—and South Los Angeles a firestorm after Rodney King, burning cross streets, Vermont and Manchester, in the city of the angels. *Ashes, ashes,*

all fall down. Church parking lot surfaced with good intents, police cars

hunkered as if smack in the Batcave, smack in an urban war zone. Lines of the hungry stretched past us, under where had been Pepperdine palms

    while *ashes, ashes, all fall down*, floating Pentecost as deadness passed

    for quiet. *Eli, Eli, lama sabachthani?* Archangel Michael stood in camo, cradling an M16 in a doorway, walls smoke and air. *Ashes, ashes, all fall*

    down. while blades revolved and passed, news copters gone existential.

Dry bones heard no Word of the Lord. Police beating Rodney, pulling over
my pastor for Driving While Black. *Eli, Eli, lama sabachthani?* The flames

while Batman hid in his cave, stores along Vermont one big sheet of flame

in the sizzle of blood, bonfire sparked of frustration. Where did the Bat go after dark? Nowhere near West L.A., yuppies in BMWs for a night of light

looting. News reported and dropped it. *Eli, Eli, lama sabachthani?* South

L.A. played easier. *Ashes, ashes, all fall down.* No day to breathe. Shadow of wings—angels, jam-jar clear, hanging around, above the bread line—

every day above ground a good time for ashes to scatter. Rest's negotiable.

Let's Take a Commercial Break Here

for Elder Zamora

You'd never searched online for those glittering
candy-hued Swarovski crystal unicorns,
manes sparking and blazing as they danced onscreen.
But there they were, as if Jeff Bezos had drilled

into your mind personally. Like my watching
the film *Miracle of the White Stallions*
and, next morning, getting an invitation
to join Equestrian Mate dot com—Santa

not giving a hang about naughty or nice
but going pure capitalist, cookies set
on a plate next to the spyware. Isn't that like
an algorithm, rummaging through the drawers

to see what's hidden under the underthings
and going spelunking into the pool of greed,
monitoring how far the ripples travel,
how deep into the credit card? You expect

Whole Foods to peddle barrels of tepache
and claim fermented pineapple punch cleanses
colons faster than a person would think to
say "cultural appropriation," lap-dancing

on a laptop until microprocessors
go tilt and a computer screen makes the sun
glitter like a diamond ring inside my head.
Like a Zales ad special. Aren't the stars jewels—

something to sell at a sunstantial profit,
substantial at a cosmic perspective?
Green with a sheen, gifts that can last a lifetime.
As another slogan goes, "I'm loving it."

A Surreal Intimacy, Like Jazz Music

                    The skunk is early. Daylight Savings Time left
it discombobulated as me, only
more outspoken in fragrant opinion. Smelling
this funk leaves a pungent smile, almost laughing.
And the coyote before sunup, sprinting
to keep out of sight and somehow find a meal.
I'm the quiet one in this relationship—

move, they think I'm about to take a solo
and fade fast, go invisible. Got to stay
the motionless pine on which ravens land and
dance, testing green limbs' springiness with weight,
needling the tree. One takes off, another lands
on or close enough to the same spot, bouncing
and heaving itself aloft. It's enough to

stay rooted. Tree and I have that much buried
in the soil between us. Sky for incentive
on the air's bluer days, regardless of clouds.
Might sound boring but it keeps me a heartbeat
when a pulse is all a person might have left.
That and a breeze circulating through the vacant
hall, dust floating between sunup and sundown.

No One Has the Last Laugh

1. With No Apologies to the World or the Ether

>the birds opened their coffee klatch in earnest,
>chatting the sky from black to blue in maybe
>a hundred singing telegrams. I sipped coffee
>
>and eavesdropped on the overlapping timbres
>and turns of phrase in their feathered acrobatics.
>Pick-up trucks grumbled past, into Wednesday,
>
>more mind-reader than machine for engines
>which sounded more like drivers' complaints
>than random idling. Amid the light twittering,
>
>a raven sounded a bass note twice. The other
>birds stopped. Paused to listen? A long silence.
>A second raven answered, more like laughing.

2. Yet Not So Dirty, Surely Not in the Spiritual Sense,

two ravens stand alfresco with a dead rat across the street median.
Asphalt may as well be fresh plaster.
Or would that be a lie?
Or are rat and birds all components of a lie,
or of an all-encompassing truth inherent in untruthing

when there's nothing but the truth on the ground?
My pastor claimed Genesis was not the book of creation,
but of recreation. This explains
the almost ritualistic ambiance which hovers over that median.
Each one stays on its designated side

as the corvids move their beaks like paintbrushes.

One picks up the carcass by the hip and drops it.
The other pulls at the rat's shoulder.
One waits for the other to finish before taking its turn,
arranging a still life that they can't keep still for the life of them.

3. The Whole Other Issue of Belonging

           holds true for an old married couple.
  A mated pair of ravens at opposite ends of a power pole's cross-tree.
        Later, they're wing to wing, rubbing beaks.
           Bickered and making up.

       Other days, one's atop the pole grooming itself
         while the other minds its own business.
      Once or twice, I've caught one grooming the other.
          They remind me of the one time

         I shaved my wife's legs at the sink.
  One of her legs propped on the sink edge, one arm around my waist.
    One of my arms around her waist, the other working the razor.
          She said I didn't cut or nick her.

4. Just So You Know, This Is the Falling-Off Place

as a squirrel hangs from its rear toes, twists a ripe persimmon
until you swear it, not the fruit, will fall from the tree. Same
rodent hops back and forth atop a power line. It never stops;
it never falls.
    A raven lands, perches on a phone pole. It caws
its solitary note Miles Davis cool. Stays static as a nevermore
Poe relation, watching the squirrel. Bird returns every day,
front row for this high-wire rodent.
        Sunday, there's a boom
like a cherry bomb. Lights go out. Squirrel's on the ground.
Later, the raven alights over the spot. It doesn't stop cawing.

Birds Make Poor Role Models

Perched on a weathered phone pole at my house, where the raven I called Miles usually sat, here was this one, *standing on the waters casting its bread*. I called the bird Jokerman, after the Dylan song. That raven became more neighbor than the clean-freak guy next door who cleaned up America one cigarette butt and stray burger wrapper after another, scavenging like ravens do.
                         Jokerman returned that day and each day after, flapping close past my head toward the pole, all the while laughing. Damned if it wasn't going to live up to the name I continued daring to call to its face—or more like its back, which it kept turned toward me.
               And damned if Jokerman didn't start walking down the center line of my street, like clean freak next door when he laid pine cones along the median so cars rocketing up or down hill would hit one, get a scare, maybe slow down. And here's that raven, gone cock of the walk, black marble eyes awhirl as its head cocked left, right, while it strutting straight down the yellow and black line— the only time Jokerman kept his beak closed.
                           Bird took to a high pine within my line of sight, went Vegas stand-up lounge lizard. It yakked nonstop, audience of one behind glass. Like clean freak, who never stopped for breath—guy was handy enough to Super Glue your ears back onto your head if they fell off and talk until they fell off again. Jokerman swooped past me, like the Vegas sign-off clean freak used at the end of a marathon chat—*I'll be here all week, enjoy the buffet.*

Like the Scream of the Rising Moon

I am still waiting for the gloaming to rip like a fabric bolt
even before it finishes unrolling from a pair
of owls slashing it top to bottom—
shrieks sharper than talons, bodies blurred
into long streaks between buildings, leaving not a whoosh

or other sound betraying pure force that almost scalped me
just going close overhead one night. A long
time after that, nothing. The other
night they were back, and I felt ice thicken
beneath my skin—the terror of unmistakable suddenness—

invisible in a sky of colors pooling together, hemorrhaging
from beak and speed. Safe under the porch
roof in waiting's stillness, watched
with a friend who thought me crazy for fear
of a bird. We'd gazed at hawks spiraling, heard eagles keen,

and when she saw the owls, her breath froze inside her chest,
observing their swift, surgical precision.
The neighbor's cat was nowhere.
Waiting, still, to catch sight of it padding
near the pomegranate tree. As if it will. As if night were still.

Followed by Periods of Silence Which Get Shorter and Shorter

It's fuck and eggs at two a.m. for these birds,
dog breath-warm air before the storm, the very
ironic-even-to-the-clock moniker

"mockingbird" showing absolute disdain for
wandering coyotes and somnolent folks
in this house. Maybe this is an avian cue

from Frank Zappa to get it on by the modus
screw-them operandi, *So who gives a fuck,
anyway*? Which is their stared intention,

though taking a fuck might have been more in mind.
Maybe they are hoping to charm statues out
of marble trees, from sitting on porcelain

with the stony countenance of not giving
a shit while giving a shit for shit's sake.
The airspace goes crapulent, diuretic

with involved warbling, a Mozartian
hard-on if ever a fuck-fest spun by the
reproductive measure, trill and mordant and

oh, let me run and screw you silly. And they
might be right. Small wonder they sound so pretty,
stuffed with operatic libido between

feathers and dawn, bones and tunes buoyant enough
to make a black- or midnight-blue morning lean,
if not to grace, then a welcome substitute.

We See One Thing Next to Another

1[1]

Wild canids that were affable, less threatening
were able to draw nearer to human communities.
They thrived on scraps, on what we threw away.
They survived better with us than without us.
We helped each other hunt. Kept each other warm.
Eventually it became a reciprocity not only
of efficiency, but of cooperation, even affection.

2[2]

Humans bond emotionally as we gaze into each
other's eyes. Such gaze-mediated bonding exists
between us and our closest animal companions,
dogs. Mutual gazing increases oxytocin levels,
and sniffing oxytocin increases gazing in dogs,
an effect that transfers to their owners. Wolves,
who rarely engage with their human handlers
in eye contact, seem resistant to this effect.

---

[1] Macgregor, Jeff. "The New Science of Our Ancient Bond with Dogs." Smithsonian Magazine, Dec 2020. https://www.smithsonianmag.com/science-nature/new-science-ancient-bond-with-dogs-180976226/. Accessed Nov 27, 2020

[2] Nagasawa, Miho, Shouhei Mitsui, Shiori En, Nobuyo Ohtani, Mitasuaki Ohta, Yasuo Sakuma, Tatsushi Onaka, Kazutaka Mogi and Takafumi Kikisui, "Oxytocin-gaze positive loop and the coevolution of human-dog bonds." *Science*, April 17, 2015 (Vol. 348, Issue 6232), pp. 333-336.

3[3]

When police retrieved the body of a man who
had committed suicide by shooting himself
in the mouth, they noticed bite marks around
what remained of his face. As they transported
his normal-acting, cooperative German shepherd
to an animal sanctuary, the dog vomited up
what was clearly his owner's skin and beard hair.

4[4]

Behaviors of 14 domestic dogs were videotaped
over a series of trials and analyzed for elements
corresponding to an owner-identified *guilty look*.
More such behaviors were seen when owners
scolded their dogs, more pronounced when dogs
were obedient, not disobedient. The guilty look
is a response to owner cues, not over a misdeed.

5[5]

From cave painting on, from Cerberus to Snoopy,
the dog is everywhere with us, in us, around us.
As a symbol of courage or loyalty, as a bad dog,
mad dog, *release the hounds* evil, the dog is

---

[3] Berman, Robby. "Dogs, cats, other pets: would they eat you if you died?" bigthink.com, June 26, 2017. https://bigthink.com/robby-berman/ever-wonder-if-your-beloved-dog-or-cat-would-eat-you-if-you-died Accessed Nov 24, 2020.

[4] Horowitz, Alexandra. "Disambiguating the 'guilty look': salient prompts to a familiar dog behavior." Pubmed.gov (National Library of Medicine, National Center for Biotechnical Information), July 2009. https://pubmed.ncbi.nlm.nih.gov/19520245/. Accessed Nov 27, 2020.

[5] Macgregor, ibid.

tightly woven into our stories, shaped in our image and likeness in a lot of ways. By knowing the dog, we know ourselves. The dog is a mirror.

There Is No Indication This Will Happen

1

Atop a power pole, a raven lets loose a white waterfall of guano when someone further uphill stops and rants at my window. No idea why he started yelling. I greet this raven every morning, speak gently, happy for the regularity of its presence. Maybe it's returning the favor. Maybe, in the corvid scheme of exterior decorating, it thinks the neighbor's looks would improve with a lighter shade of make-up. Something between Kabuki and Killer Klown. The black bird turns toward me. Clicks and pops a message that could mean, "You're welcome. Go enjoy your coffee. I'll see you tomorrow."

2

There were 24 of them. Skeletons in graves, between 4500 and 5000 years old. Damaged lower vertebrae. Thickened pelvic bones. Ridged femurs. Day-in, day-out price, learning how to ride horses across deep-green European grass steppes. How many hundreds of times were they thrown? How many pulled muscles? Twisted ligaments? Or, since these men rode atop the beast's hind end, not its back, sore posteriors from harder bouncing through the day. And which was first and, at the end of the day, a pain to whom—horse to rider or rider to horse? Do bony hands across crotches suggest a toll?

3

When will we get *Watergate: The Rock Opera*? Elvis Presley as special guest, offering a fried peanut butter, banana and bacon sandwich in place of cottage cheese and ketchup as I Am Not a Crook in Chief's final meal in office. Elvis saying, "You're no hound dog, boss." Quick scene change. Nixon dressed as Cleopatra. Centurions entering his chamber with an asp, singing, in chorus, Lennon and McCartney's "With a Little Help from My Friends." Tricky Dick responding with Clarence Carter, wanting to get lost in their rock-and-roll and drift away. Throwing his shoulders back. Remembering he's a Nile queen.

4

"He didn't piss on top of the roof," my neighbor told me. "He walked to the top step and let go, facing your window. Brightest yellow I'd seen." Would've been better, I thought, if it had been beer, but couldn't see our mutual friend wasting anything undrunk on me. My neighbor continued: "Asked me if I had a Glo-Stick. Said he wanted to wrap it like a snake around his penis so you'd see what he was doing. Is blue still your favorite color? Just wondered. If you've got time, could you pick up a 12-pack of Tecate Light?"

5

My mom dreamed, just after my great-grandfather died, about standing in the kitchen he'd handcrafted for my great-grandmother. Gleaming white cabinetry. Some doors no bigger than a cuckoo clock. Tiny latch-handles like crosses, waiting to be turned. She turned and there he stood. Long-sleeve khaki shirt and trousers as usual. Didn't say if he also had on his hat to go outside. Before she said anything, he put a finger to his lips and disappeared. His way of saying goodbye, she said. How many times since she passed have I wished he'd shown her how to do that with me?

We All Came to Be Here Quite Naturally
after the painting Women in Black *by Marianne von Werefkin*

The women haul sacks across their backs, filled with lives.
Black scarves on heads. Black aprons over indigo dresses.
They resemble ravens as they walk in a line to the riverbank.

the hue of routine, the hue of loss, hue of the world added,

the smell of blood and earth captured between themselves.
Two commiserate as they scrub, rinsing fabric and fabric.
One hauls a wet sack out of sight, face turned out of view,

carting what can't be let go for the fear its weight belongs,

The bag's white canvas could pass for a fallen companion,
the way she lugs it, pulled close to her side, not letting go.
The nearby mountain's deep blue overshadows the village.

    Home is dust returning to dust. Home stares in the mirror.
    Home is a scarf, keeping what's under it neat and hidden.
    Home's a raven group called a rave, called an unkindness—

*   inevitability of rest and rest, place and living what remains,*

    —and if crows instead of ravens, a group would be a murder.
    Not grieving is murder. As if God told Werefkin's women,
    "Your brother's blood cries our to Me from the ground."

The mountain looms behind the village, heavy with bones,
and dominates the painting. At its base, the stream glows.
Sun bleeds light into the sky, bleaching a peak further off

leaving the valley's deep blue sigh which also has its place,

while reddening other slopes behind, another hint of blood

and a redness of earth tasted in a Russian heirloom tomato.
The far-off peak's auburn could pass for dried onion roots,

the body's slowdown despite the muscle-memory of routine,

as I chop onion for stew and think of Werefkin's painting—
the sulfurous bite to nostrils and earth under which it grew,
and a morning more slate than robin in its chilled overcast

expected and also belonging, more thanks to time than place

My wife opens her late sister's travel bag from the hospital,
filled with teddy bears and unicorns. A flash-flood of tears.
She has me throw it away. The hurt cannot be thrown away.

    Ashes—a small scattering—go beneath a yellow rosebush.
Her sister's favorite color. That song about a ribbon on a tree.
    My wife's been listening a lot to "The Sounds of Silence,"

soles aware of pressure and pain, but a heart much more so.

    A tone not far removed from the music seeps through cloth.
What weight is the world on a bird, even if the bird is black?
    Memory can rip a sack by its weight, can overflow and spill

How much grief becomes home? How much becomes bone?
If the women's garments became raven wings, would they fly?
Would my wife choose the air with her heart a broken wing?

in the ongoing steps along a path worn smooth, packed hard.

The woman arrive at the stream amid a conspiracy of ravens.
They remind me of ravens around water, looking at reflections.
They women wash clothes so as not to see what haunts them,

carving a place as years shorten steps, sun lengthens in sky,

but notice nonetheless what has made home on their faces,
creaks before dawn in muscles, almost in tune with the land.
The earth groans as sole becomes soul. Penance wears soil.

A sack rips. Weight of mother and sister borne from childhood.
   Or fabric of a tarp spread where my wife's sister was staying
  when she couldn't get to the bathroom. We brought her home,

fulfilling a longing which never really washes away, belonging,

The tarp was blue plastic—the hue of Werefkin's mountain—
and it shimmered like water in morning light as she shambled
but stood straight, not hunched like the women in the painting.

Home is memory's unkindness while raving to distinguish
anything close to reason, settling for black homespun fabric,
secured with hooks and eyes instead of buttons' uncertainty

stubborn as a dull ache and stiffness in legs, feet, shoulders,

in place and time from this scene and so much of it as well,
threading a vine of perspective toward the women, the trek,
a taste for purple tomatoes, their taste of sun predominant

ever present despite the season's snow, mountains' altitude,

my wife's playing "The Sounds of Silence" on laundry day
expected as inhalation as field becomes town, becomes birch
protecting town, the grove white-barked, mute and attentive,

walking until indelible as the stone-grey houses, white snow,

beguiling as jam—and erosive as jam on teeth for what loss
they may contain inside while birches watch the procession,
quake from heaviness contained in sacks as the women pass.

Like the Cubist Diary of a Brook

> *California has joined a growing number of states that allow residents to compost their bodies after death.*
> —*Sarah Kuta*, Smithsonian Magazine

Let me become a tree part
concealed in bark and leaf part
sandwiched between rings between

    I paint

between seen and known in wind
babbling through the greening
canopy its breathing then

    paint objects as

then and nowness a clear stream
burbling past limb and trunk
let me become a tree lay

    as I

lay a month in alfalfa
wood chips and used coffee grounds
as a tribute to the joke

    I think them not

joke my blood type is French roast
running astrological
risk of my sign being read

    not as I

read as a Starbucks logo
lay me in alfalfa wood
chips straw in a steel bathtub

I see them I paint

bathtub take me away one
long Calgon moment let me
molder in clover Calgon take

paint objects

take me away that old ad line
I must be brain-dead to quote
it but it's my hay pile and

objects not as I

and I'll rot if I want to
a month of budding microbes
of summer days spread to pun

I see

pun curing a cadaver
of cadaving to mix remains
thoroughly with ground to plant

see them I paint objects as I think

plant for rest and shade instead
of lawns dotted with headstones
imagine Sherwood Forest

think them not as I

Forest oaks elms sycamores
from Errol Flynn's *Robin Hood*
wave after wave of trees bend

I see them

bend and a waterfall from

the roar cascading past leaves as
limbs shadow what was what grows

It Must Mean I'm Not Here Yet

Memories are meant to be
glared at. Like this exercise
class—is it Stretch & Flex or
Bend & Mend? Or is concrete
the flavor of the sky? It's

so crunchy, like eggshells in
cumulus meringue. Not doom's
heliotrope but kudzu
crams its way through every spare
thought with tendrils. Lavender

sprigs surface in sea green tide.
Heart shaped imaginations
in the imaginer's field
pose as leaves, fresh from the dread
of Joe's Garage. Borage blooms,

blue and purple, descend as if
stars from sky. Watermelons,
pre-Easter gray, wait graveside
for paint, to be made festive.
"Imaginary songs sound

best," Joe says, "from the heart of
a Fender Stratocaster."
Willow branches bend as if
the tree listens and weeps
green along the kudzu sea.

Our Quondam Companions Persist

Of my country and of my family I
have little to say that hasn't been either
rent or splattered upon. Bone fragments and dots
of brain create paisley Rorschach patterns in

the fabric of my conscience. Let's allot the
dappled cotton skein to drape figures gone
more statue than statuesque. Children, how you
bleed. You shape garnet- and wine-colored mud pies

and smear them against your faces and clothes
to blend with earth, ashes to ashes, bullets
to dust, all the pretty bodies going down.

This Future Does Us Good ("Lawful and Proper"[6])

Let's pepper spray children, so we might act
swiftly on Swift's modest proposal and devour
our protests of incongruity. This proposal may

seem unpalatable to some, perhaps to many,
but the hood is lovely, dark and deep and we
have promises to keep, lawful and proper

with proper seasoning and served on a bed
of sauteed guile. Yes, we realize mothers may
push representatives of law enforcement away

from their offspring, that the boys and girls
may improve their muscle tone and thus add
entertainment and flavor to the proceedings—

and they should proceed. By all means, let
officers swing high and mighty their batons,
for singles, doubles, home runs are warranted

this season before the playoffs, for which
Mookie Betts made good go west, young man,
in the sports equivalent of manifest destiny

while other young Black men were perforated
and suffocated at traffic stops and domestic
interludes of disputes. Are you not entertained?

---

[6] Words used by the Seattle Police Department's Office of Police Accountability over the pepper-spraying of children by officers during a May 30 Black Lives Matter protest. (Link to article: https://www.nydailynews.com/news/national/ny-seattle-police-pepper-spraying-of-child-found-to-be-lawful-20200918-dkx6twbtknhw5gyxpuglfnpcja-story.html

Supposing That You Are a Wall

It's the second cup which fills cracks in the mortar of myself, black
and unsweetened but with the familiar woodiness which is coffee,

and I recall black-and-white footage of Robert Frost making java—

boiling milk, pouring the saucepan into some instant at the bottom
of a glass—mending a wall as he took a long sip between the world

    and never really knowing what cat or crazy man is going to crash in,
    cracking white wooden pickets, pulling stones in a wall out of place,

    whether rounded stones with the heft of baseballs or an angular hunk,

    as my eye follows cracks like hinges or zippers between red bricks—
    depending if composure bends or comes undone—in retaining walls

which might as well hold back the ocean and in truth actually do so,
unless another earthquake stoves in the hillside—a tectonic widening

of perspective deeper than misgivings, as if the planet's bones crack

and numbers widen on a clock face like pizza dough or a Dali reject.
My rafters shake, reverberant in one California stereotype or another

    as a nearby police helicopter loop-de-loops, and three news choppers
    hover over a car chase, like one more brick in Pink Floyd's wall. Do

    any nearby donut shops brew more joe while the officers motor in—

    maybe even thankful, steaming stillness cupped in hands as they sit,
    impassive, contoured in booths like pavers mortared into patterns—

while I scoop grounds into a paper filter and wait, thinking of woods
lovely dark and deep—as if there were anything darker than promises

compelled to keep—aroma from the kitchen not pine or sycamore—

and a deep dark settling, holding so many bricks of morning in place,
into a stillness which passes for solid and earthen, at least for a while.

The Lady of Shalott's in Hot Water Again

That's how it's told from the male-centric perspective, the guy who tells what he insists is the story. She's cursed
                                       if she pauses from her weaving
to look outside, but she has no clue what that curse might be. She hangs a mirror to look outside,
                    working the loom with her feet as she stretches
to pound a nail into a wall to suspend the looking glass and our disbelief while the wooden loom jostles and hums
                             because women do everything
except spot a gap in logic sure as light through a thinning patch of fabric whose threads while the bolt stretched from the loom were always awry.

✦

Narrator—male—says it's her fault, when Lancelot flashed in the mirror, bright as a sunbeam and tall in the saddle,
                             that the Lady just had to look.
The mirror cracked and the spell of protection gushed away like a split seam in Titanic's hull
                 when it got that cold shoulder. Mixing metaphors
but she was just as doomed as the liner and doom is doom for a woman—who splits hairs or dust bunnies on that one?
                                   Dumb bunny, Anne Sexton
said about Snow White. It's meta but a wonder about fairy tale heroines, how they make it to the end. Doesn't happen in my deep concrete forest.

✦

She looked straight toward Camelot, got cold-cocked by flying dementia. Never mind Lancelot stalking her, sunlight
                                   timed to glint from his armor
into said looking glass. Plot device out of a Lifetime movie. Spell broke, along with her ankle.

                      Doctor said it was all just a sprain—her rationality would heal just fine. She ambled three weeks in pain and a blissful state, thanks to new medication—when a man
                                        doubts a woman, prescribe pills. Like when a man doubts a woman caught inside reflections, running into glass recollections which shatter upon impact. "He's a knight, after all."

✦

Either meds or a mild concussion got the Lady to think about seeking the Holy Grail. Forget second opinions. She
                                  thirsted for Casablanca— to drink from the waters—but misinformed on liquid assets. Lancelot followed her. He was
                  a ringer for Humphrey Bogart, cigarette smoke wreathing around him like a pet cobra. Narrator didn't want Lancelot to come across as the Marlboro Man, riding
                                high with smoker's cough and getting lung cancer—tarnishes a knight's repute, Not to mention an EBT card between his nicotine-stained fingers or his thinning hair—

✦

as if the Round Table gave federal assistance. And there was something predatory about those soulful brown eyes,
                              something serpentine, coiled within metallic scales to strike. Who'd believe King Arthur's man would not treat a woman ladylike?
                    That was the point—ladylike lies in the eye of the withholder, all secrets and cries in secluded spaces—repute never in dispute. He nursed Scotch from a booth
                            as the Lady, from a bar stool, offered whoever stopped to order drinks the directions to hell and back. Swore the directions were good. Follow them, you'd only get lost twice.

Hence It Ends Up with a Scenario of Them All Getting Paid
after the painting La Culture des Idées *by René Magritte*

1

All the polished, gleaming pipes
seem lies as they lie about,
seeking in their poison whom
in leonine tawniness
they may well devour. Ceci

n'est pas une pipe. Long mint-green
bird-of-paradise leaves and
those pipes of bird's heads. As if
heaven really were what you
lit in a pipe and inhaled

deep as the mahogany
brown vase, glazed and glistening
in what Magritte suggests is
cool morning light, with its haze
of not-quite-realized truth—

pretense of a pretense to
one, gospel to another.
As if that second person
had walked the Tuesday last on
water not frozen, smoking

as hell froze over, gained an
ice-skate conglomerate which
boomed, a marketing campaign
that Satan had changed his name
to Santa. Amazing what

transposing notions can make.
A public relations coup
and thaw amid a deep freeze—
a promise made in poison,
whatever your opioid.

2

Ceci n'est pas une pipe—
the eternal feminine
to hold, to damn, to cherish
in language that insists on
petticoats and petit fours

in black-and-blue derisions.
Skirts in their volume and length
hiding swollen ankles, white
plaster casts and elastic
bandages from all the trips

and falls, attempting to climb
whatever staircase you choose.
There are so many. You'd think
age makes a cliché. But there's
such good sport being sexist—

like Seurat's scene at the Seine,
all dots and poised figures, hats
and parasols included.
A decent French mise-en-scène.
To which Magritte, much like his

fellow countryman, Poirot,
might respond, "It is very
charming. But I am Belgian.
Do you have a light? I have
misplaced my propriety."

3

Perhaps it really does come
down to what wafting sky-blue
smoke gets in your vision—I
was going to say "eyes" but
that's a song and there's so much

more than that to this matter,
which is itself not matter
and fully material.
Looting the bank to get gas,
pay the grocer at check-out—

oh, what a pun for the time,
"check-out." Putting in and
smoking what no bird of
paradise takes into its
incredulity. "Are my

eyes really brown?" Rick asked in
Casablanca, reading the
little tan Nazi notebook
that was his personal file.
Yes, that was a movie but

polished and reminiscent
of thick pipe smoke and good wars,
before the rocket's scarlet
got too liquid, so glaring,
and toilet paper went scarce.

4

"They're on a table, you know,"
those pipes of paradise, not
on a white tile window-sill
but displayed nonetheless for
hundreds of container ships

floating in respective baths
and the Teamsters said we don't
tread water, not if Jesus
really were Jimmy Hoffa—
the long sheen and oily touch

in the night's cry, good as twin-
ply currency in the last-
minute distribution thing,
leaving store shelves gaping, all
those wide-open wounds to feed—

good as the sea releasing
its dead to the check-out line,
flooding the supermarkets
while the pipes leaf out and stretch
toward heaven. So many

serpents or eagle-looking
vultures gleaming ceramic
in marble obstinacy.
A sole red tulip shares room
with clashing philosophies.

5

That flower. Exhibited
for matinees and late nights.
Shows Death, on his pale Harley,
likes to see something pretty
and carmine when he rolls in,

past the hedge on the other
side of the bomb-blasted mall,
having picked up a bargain.
Got to love the water marks
under that vase, the blotter—

all that red deepened to black.
Old blood soaked into bandage?
Hemorrhaging ledger? All
that is read and isn't red—
ceci n'est pas rouge? Long leaves

rustle. Hint of pipe smoke or
wormwood in the corner back
of my eyes. Wafts of sage, thyme,
rosemary. Wormwood bites, though.
Hits the tongue and doesn't stop.

There Had Never Been a Problem with the Water Before[7]

1[8]

A datura plant with creamy white blossoms
grows between the legs of a half-buried beach
chair. A sunken boat turns to bones. A story
from the Hopi says that the previous world
also flooded. People who escaped made
it rising on a reed boat or by climbing
a ladder. Where the cliff went underwater,
ladders pecked into the rock turned green under
the surface, then black, then disappeared—tip of
a shadow-nicked ladder leaning against rock.

2[9]

We use the term Mother Earth. But Mother Earth
is a blue planet. Water is not blue; we
see it as blue. Amniotic fluid has
about 2% salinity. Oceans
are 3.0 to 3.5% dissolved salts.
All life seems to have come from the ocean, but
all life does not carry some sort of ancient,
immutable salt signature. Water is
the thinnest of layers on the surface of the
planet. Water is precious. Water is life.

---

[7] Title taken from the poem "Coma Berenices" by John Ashbery, in the collection *Where Shall I Wander*.

[8] Source: Childs, Craig. "The Return of Glen Canyon." *Atlas Obscura*, March 6, 2023. https://www.atlasobscura.com/articles/glen-canyon-lake-powell-drought Accessed March 10, 2023.

[9] Source: Author cited as womenslegacy. "Oceans and Amniotic Fluid" womenslegacyproject.com, April 22, 2020. https://womenslegacyproject.com/our-collective-legacy/oceans-and-amniotic-fluid/ Accessed March 10, 2023.

3[10]

There is no life in thee now, except rocking
imparted by a gentle rolling ship, by
her, borrowed from the sea, by the sea, from the
inscrutable tides of God. But while this sleep,
this dream is on thee, move your foot or hand an
inch, slip your hold at all, and identity
comes back in horror. Over Descartian
vortices you hover. And perhaps, at midday,
in the fairest weather, with one half-throated
shriek you drop, no more to rise for ever.

4[11]

The power had been out for a week, snow to
the rafters. Neighbors found 94-year-old
"Dolly" bundled up in a chair in front of her
fireplace, which had gone cold. Alden Park Thayer,
85, died as the snow drifts outside piled
up to 10 feet, then 14 feet. His daughter,
snowed in with his body for days, was keeping
a wary eye on fine cracks in her ceiling
that appeared after the blizzard heaped snow on-
to her roof. She was trying not to panic.

---

[10] Source: Melville, Herman. "Chapter 35: The Mast-head." Moby Dick. https://etc.usf.edu/lit2go/42/moby-dick/693/chapter-35-the-mast-head/ Accessed March 10, 2023.

[11] Source: Hubler, Shawn and Jill Cowan. "Residents Fret Over Deaths in Southern California Mountains." *The New York Times*, March 9, 2023. https://www.nytimes.com/2023/03/09/us/san-bernardino-snow-deaths.html Accessed March 10, 2023.

5[12]

There is the crumpling, the mess. A marina
that once floated in a cove has been towed out
of the shrinking lake and dropped in a field of
Russian thistle, metal pontoons partially
sunk into dry, crack-crazed soil. Cooler doors stand
open—the marina was once known for its
ice cream—and conduits hang from ceilings, wires
stripped. Cove it once occupied is disappearing,
turning back into land as lake levels fall.
Only one boat ramp is still operable

---

[12] Source: Childs.

Waiters Encourage Us, and Squirrels

                          scamper, hoarding broomcorn,
                            sawtoothing sunflower seeds,
                        out of greed as much as nutrition.
                              Is it really as unpretentious
                      as scattered food-stained napkins
                      and latte-scented paper cups,

                    rolled onto random recollections,
                            washed with rainwater
                  toward a kaleidoscope plastic ocean
                              lethargic as pond scum?
                            It's like something
                      our parents may have told us,

loud and long, "Clean up your room!"
                        I bulldozed a garbage yard
                into nether regions beneath my bed
                          so Mom would let me shop
                  for a plastic model car. Didn't know
                  I was being so adult and millennial,

                                a generation or two
                before bright red, sky and navy blues
                          and clear as no bell
                I could imagine Glad Wrap to sound—
                        all glittery and suffocating,
                  and all of it putting a toxic spin

                on the name Pacific, gulls and whales
                    stuffed tight tasting the rainbow.
                I'm thinking of the squirrels again,
                    picking up and devouring
                what feels like hours, as if anyone
                    could taste time, let alone

                starve from the lack of it. As if
                      we could all be cooks
                and eat our mistakes. We're more

like John-Boy Walton on *Night Gallery*,
a sin-eater's son
substituting for his ill father,

wailing long lamentations
as he cleared away a rich-man's feast
out of sight behind a closed door,
no crumb to his lips
just as his mother had told him,
squirreling it home—

only to find it laid before his father's corpse,
the son having to consume
uncountable lifetimes of moral refuge
his father had devoured, all of it
wrapped in spiced meats, bread, cakes.
The squirrels and my obsessive neighbor

might have the right idea, collecting
crimes and missed demeanors like seeds.
And seeds they are—weeds or vines
of aluminum, plastic, desiccated tree,
which snowflake as if bread crumbs
onto white linen, left abandoned

for a waiter's metal tool to whisk away.

Pierced Full of Holes by the Evil That Is Not Evil

It's like the message I got from a church friend,
about how I was becoming increasingly liberal,
like some blossoming magnolia tree whose bark
was becoming patched with rust or blight. I look
at photographs and video of National Guardsmen

sleeping on the marble floor of the U.S. Capitol,
motionless as piles of autumn leaves, camouflage
blotches of fatigues and backpacks only adding
incongruences of a forest growing out of stone.
I think of Santa Anita Canyon, where bush maples

split granite boulders as they press upward. Those
trees had reminded me before now of resilience—
that even with only a toehold onto which to cling,
I could pull myself from depression, not plummet
isolated to smash below. Maybe a selfish notion—

those roots still force themselves, pry things apart
to assert themselves, spread and deepen their hold.
You expect me next to mention the screaming mass
at the Capitol, who seeded the forest of Guardsmen,
blowing ice shards, clouds of pepper spray in their

winter storm? Or the faceless, helmeted, Kevlar-clad
lines of authority shadowing masses who shouted
Black lives matter in heated gusts over summer—
not orange-gold of acres of trees going up at once,
a fire-beast seeming to inhale whole counties, exhale

heaps of powdered ash. Nor was it a controlled burn—
is controlled pulling over folks for driving while black,
like shaking trees until the leaves drop, stay stock-still,
and trunks smile daylight? It's controlling, like seeing
a match or candle gutter out as what little air or fuel

is left inside of it dissipates. But is a tapir controlled?
Merely abandoned? Abandonment blazed. Travelled

in sparks and embers and Clown, emissary of chaos,
said this fire was bad. Bad for being a cleansing fire?
For hungering to devour brush along the forest floor,

thorns which drew blood? For finding thick glades
between tall buildings, pools of dried blood sunk
between pieces of gravel in asphalt? Guardsmen
sleep and I think of smatterings of scarlet, yellow,
brown in the gutter of a winding mountain road—

how Clown said there was nothing evil in winter,
a storm is a storm is a storm. But in which rustle
is good or bad? In what crack spreading in stone?
Clown told us before we should be raking leaves,
as if a rake's metallic scratch could stop the wind.

Acknowledgements

I am grateful to the editors of the following journals in which the following poems have appeared, sometimes in different versions and under different titles:

Book of Matches: "Appearances Must Be Kept Up at Whatever Cost Until the Day of Judgment and Afterward If Possible"; "We See One Thing Next to Another"

GLEAM: Journal of the Cadralor: "Pondering a Theorum: What You Said a Hotel Was"

MacQueen's Quinterly: "A Surreal Intimacy, Like Jazz Music"; "Followed by Periods of Silence Which Get Shorter and Shorter"; "Hence It Ends Up with a Scenario of Them All Getting Paid"; "It Belongs to Each of Us Like a Blanket"; "It Must Mean I'm Not Here Yet"; "Like the Cubist Diary of a Brook"; "The Whole Other Issue of Belonging"; "There had Never Been a Problem with the Water Before"; "There Is No Indication This Will Happen"; "Yet Not So Dirty, Surely Not in a Spiritual Sense"

Rise Up Review: "This Future Does Us Good ('Lawful and Proper')"

Synkroniciti: "Batman Came Out and Clubbed Me"; "Birds Make Poor Role Models"; "Just So You Know, This Is the Falling-Off Place"; "Make Nice, Like You Really Cared"; "Only the Frozen Emphasis"; "Pierced Full of Holes by the Evil That Is Not Evil"; "Supposing You Are a Wall"; "The Lady of Shalott's in Hot Water Again"; "We All Came to Be Here Quite Naturally"

The New Verse News: "Our Quondam Companions Persist"

Verse Virtual: "And Toward the Center a Vacancy One Knew"

"Like the Scream of the Rising Moon" appeared in the Silver Birch Press blog series *I Am Still Waiting* on April 26, 2021.

"There Are Always Those Who Think You Ought To" appeared in the anthology *Insurrection* by Gnashing Teeth Publishing.

"Waiters Encourage Us, and Squirrels" appeared in the Silver Birch Press blog series *How to Heal the Earth* on December 6, 2021.

"With No Apologies to the Word or the Ether" was Poem of the Day at Gnashing Teeth Publishing on April 1, 2021.

About the Author

Jonathan Yungkans is currently an in-home care provider and types in the wee hours while watching a skunk wander under his house. He is thankful when his writing is less noxious than that creature's calling card. In other guises, he has been a mental-health support-group moderator, teacher, delivery driver and publications editor. He lives in Whittier, California.

www.ingramcontent.com/pod-product-compliance
Lightning Source LLC
LaVergne TN
LVHW050029080526
838202LV00070B/6979